Embers of Resilience
Finding Strength in Adversity.

Lois D. Kroger

INTRODUCTION.

Every thread in the life tapestry represents a happy, sad, successful, or unsuccessful moment. Every thread comes together to create the elaborate and distinctive pattern that is each of our journeys. Resilience is the common thread that unites all of us in this magnificent tapestry.

Every person has an ember of resilience waiting to light when they are exposed to adversity. We can weather life's storms, rise from the ashes of adversity, and emerge stronger and wiser because of our intangible strength.

"Embers of Resilience," this book, explores that subtle, yet powerful force that exists within each of us. To discover the mysteries of resilience, we will travel together through the valleys of vulnerability, the peaks of fortitude, and the alleys of understanding. We will come across inspirational people who have fanned the flames of their courage and determination.

As we set out on this journey, keep in mind that resilience is a trait shared by many, not just a few. It's a talent, an art form that each of us can develop, hone, and apply. The tactics and tales presented in the ensuing pages serve as your manual, your arsenal, and your source of inspiration.

Now, let's set out on a journey to discover the core of resilience and the ember that can fan the strongest flames of hope, tenacity, and unwavering strength.

CHAPTER 1
Understanding Resilience.

Resilience is a broad term that includes the capacity to bear hardship, overcome obstacles, and turn adversity into opportunity. It entails adapting and becoming stronger in the face of difficulties; it goes beyond simply getting back up after a setback. We must investigate resilience's essential elements and dimensions to completely comprehend it:

1. Adaptive Coping Techniques: When faced with hardship, resilient people frequently employ adaptive coping techniques. Instead of ignoring or avoiding stressors, these strategies entail actively addressing and managing them. They might turn to others for support, change the way they see things, and concentrate on solving problems.

2. Positive Mentality: A resilient mentality entails keeping an optimistic attitude despite difficult circumstances. It all comes down to viewing challenges as chances for improvement, education, and self-improvement. People with resilience frequently have faith in their capacity to overcome challenges.

3. Emotional Intelligence: The capacity to identify, comprehend, and control one's own emotions as well as those of others is a key component of emotional intelligence, which is strongly related to resilience. People with higher emotional intelligence are better able to handle difficulty and remain composed.

4. Supportive Social Networks: Resilience can be greatly enhanced by robust social support networks. Having community, family, or friends to turn to in hard times gives one a sense of support and belonging. People who have these connections may be able to handle stress better.

5. Neuroplasticity: One of the main tenets of resilience is the brain's ability to change and reorganize itself. In response to stress, the brain can reorganize its functions and create new neural connections thanks to this ability, which promotes personal development and adaptation.

6. Personal Growth and Learning: Being resilient entails making a commitment to one's development and learning from experiences, even in the face of difficult or upsetting circumstances. It's about learning important lessons and changing as a consequence.

7. Stress Management: Resilient People frequently have well-functioning stress management techniques. They can handle a lot of stress without getting overwhelmed. This entails identifying stressors and putting strategies in place to lessen their effects.

8. Genetic and Environmental Factors: Genetic factors can affect resilience because certain people may naturally be more resilient than others. Resilience is also greatly influenced by one's experiences in life and surroundings. One's capacity to handle difficulties in the future can be improved by overcoming past setbacks.

9. Self-Compassion: Even in the face of setbacks or difficulties, resilient people frequently show kindness and compassion to themselves. Self-compassion promotes emotional well-being and acts as a protective barrier against the damaging effects of stress.

10. Resilience and Adaptability: Being resilient means being able to adjust and be flexible when things change. It's the capacity to successfully negotiate changes and adapt to novel situations.

Gaining an understanding of these essential elements and aspects of resilience offers a thorough understanding of resilience. People can overcome hardship and grow as a result of a complex interaction of psychological, emotional, social, and neurological factors.

Defining Resilience.

Resilience is a complex and important psychological quality that reflects a person's ability to tolerate and adjust to hardship, stress, trauma, or major life transitions. It's the capacity to recover from trying circumstances, frequently doing so with greater fortitude and development than just getting back to one's pre-crisis level. A resilient person is defined by:

1. Emotional Stability: Resilient People possess a strong emotional base that allows them to effectively control and regulate their emotions, particularly in trying circumstances.

2. Adaptive Coping: Using adaptive coping mechanisms in the face of adversity is a key component of resilience. In contrast to avoidance or denial, this entails proactively addressing and managing stressors, getting support, and solving problems.

3. Positive Mindset: A positive perspective on life is linked to resilience. Adversity is often seen by resilient individuals as a chance for personal development, with difficulties being temporary and manageable.

4. Perseverance: Being resilient frequently means having the willpower to carry on in the face of difficulty. Resilient people don't easily give up, even in the face of seemingly insurmountable challenges.

5. Self-Belief: Resilient People have faith in their capacity to triumph over hardship. This self-belief is essential to their ability to overcome obstacles.

6. Resourcefulness: The capacity to make efficient use of resources and adjust to changing conditions is a key component of resilience.

7. Learning and Development: Being resilient means not only getting back up after setbacks but also developing through them. It entails learning important lessons and applying them to adjust and advance.

8. Genetic and Environmental Factors: Resilience may have both genetic and environmental components, in addition to being cultivated and enhanced. While some people may be more resilient by nature, resilience can be greatly shaped by experiences in life and the environment.

Resilience is essentially a dynamic and multifaceted trait that enables people to overcome obstacles in life, come out stronger and wiser from hardship, and carry on living a fulfilling life. It is a skill that can be strengthened and developed over time rather than a fixed attribute, giving people the ability to confront and overcome the most difficult challenges in life.

The Science of Resilience.

The concept of resilience is not limited to psychology; it has a scientific basis that explores the complex interactions between the human mind and body. Comprehending the science of resilience facilitates an understanding of the neurological and psychological mechanisms that support this essential characteristic. The following are important facets of resilience science:

1. Neuroplasticity: Resilience and the brain's remarkable capacity for neuroplasticity are closely related. This is the brain's capacity to change and reorganize its wiring in response to novel situations and difficulties. It makes it possible for the brain to reorganize its functions and create new neural connections, which promotes personal development and adaptation.

2. Stress Response: People's resilience is greatly influenced by their ability to cope with stress, which is an inevitable aspect of life. Stress causes the body to release hormones that impact different body systems, such as cortisol and adrenaline. To develop resilience, one must learn to control and modulate the body's stress response.

3. Emotional Control: Resilient People frequently possess a higher degree of emotional control. This entails effectively identifying, comprehending, and controlling their emotional reactions. Resilience and emotion regulation go hand in hand because they both enable people to remain composed and make sensible choices under pressure.

4. Adaptive Coping Strategies: The study of resilience looks at the mental and physical coping mechanisms resilient people employ in the face of difficulty. These tactics include rephrasing situations in a positive light, looking for social support, solving problems, and finding significance in trying circumstances.

5. Psychological Flexibility: Adapting to shifting conditions and viewpoints is a sign of psychological flexibility, which is linked to resilience. It entails having the ability to change one's perspective, objectives, or actions in reaction to fresh knowledge or difficulties.

6. Biology and Genetics: Research indicates that a person's propensity for resilience may be influenced by their genetic makeup. The way the brain reacts to stress and adversity may be influenced by specific genetic factors.

7. Hormonal Balance: An individual's resilience can be impacted by hormones, especially those linked to stress. Part of the science of resilience involves comprehending how hormones like oxytocin and cortisol affect how the body reacts to stress.

8. Psychological Factors: The science of resilience includes cognitive elements such as a growth mindset, optimism, and self-efficacy (belief in one's abilities). These elements influence a person's capacity to prosper in the face of difficulty.

We can better understand the complex interactions between neurological, psychological, and physiological processes that underpin this crucial quality by exploring the science of resilience. With this understanding, we can not only comprehend resilience more fully but also create plans for improving it in our own and other people's lives.

Factors That Influence Resilience.

A complex characteristic, resilience is impacted by several situational, genetic, environmental, and individual factors. Gaining insight into these elements can enable us to better understand the dynamics that influence an individual's ability to overcome hardship and prosper. The following are significant determinants of resilience:

- **Genetics:** Resilience in certain individuals may have a hereditary component. Certain genes are associated with both the ability to respond to stress and solve problems. Resilience, however, can be strengthened and developed independent of genetic makeup. Genetics is but one component of the whole picture.

- **Environment and Upbringing:** Resilience can be greatly impacted by early life experiences as well as the caliber of one's upbringing. Resilience can be fostered by a loving and caring childhood environment where kids learn how to overcome hardships and establish a sense of worth.

- **Life Experiences:** Resilience can be enhanced or weakened by prior experiences, particularly traumatic ones. Overcoming hardships in the past can give people the abilities and perspective needed to deal with challenges in the future with more resilience.

- **Social Support:** One of the most important components of resilience is having a robust social support system. Relationships with friends, family, and the community offer people a sense of belonging, emotional support, and encouragement that can help them deal with stress and hardship.

- **Education and Skills:** Getting an education and learning life skills can help build resilience. Acquiring problem-solving skills, emotional control, and useful coping mechanisms can improve one's capacity to recover from setbacks.

- **Cultural and Societal Factors:** People's perspectives on and reactions to adversity can be influenced by cultural and societal norms and values. Resilience and coping mechanisms may be highly valued in some cultures as integral components of their shared identity.

- **Personal Mindset:** Resilience can be greatly influenced by an individual's mindset, which includes elements like optimism, self-efficacy (belief in one's abilities), and a growth mindset (belief that intelligence and abilities can be developed). Resilience can be strengthened by having a positive mindset and self-belief.

- **Exposure to Diversity and Adversity:** Both encountering adversity and being exposed to a range of viewpoints and experiences can help people become more resilient by extending their perspective on the world and enhancing their capacity for situational adaptation.

- **Socioeconomic and Economic Factors:** Resource availability and economic stability can affect resilience. Reducing stresses that could weaken resilience is possible when basic needs are met, healthcare is accessible, and finances are secure.

- **Health and Well-Being:** Resilience is greatly influenced by both physical and mental health. Being in good physical and mental health lays the groundwork for managing life's obstacles.

- **Attachment Style:** Resilience may be impacted by attachment styles that are shaped in early relationships. Greater emotional control and coping mechanisms in adulthood can result from secure attachments formed during childhood.

- **Adaptive Coping Strategies:** Resilience can be strengthened by the use of successful coping mechanisms like problem-solving, reaching out for social support, and rephrasing unpleasant experiences.

Building and maintaining resilience requires an understanding of these many elements and how they interact. It's crucial to remember that resilience is a skill that can be developed over time with the correct techniques and assistance; it's not a fixed attribute.

CHAPTER 2

The Roots of Adversity

A necessary component of the human experience is adversity. It includes all of the obstacles, failures, struggles, and miseries people face in their lifetimes. Comprehending the origins of adversity enables us to value the various origins and manifestations of difficulties individuals encounter. Key elements of the causes of adversity are as follows:

1. Life Transitions: Adversity can arise from any number of the transitions that occur throughout life. Moving to a new city, beginning a new job, going through a breakup or divorce, or going through significant life events like marriage, parenthood, or retirement are examples of these transitions.

2. Health Challenges: Adversity related to one's health can encompass both mental and physical health issues. It can include mental health issues like anxiety, depression, or trauma in addition to long-term sicknesses, wounds, and impairments.

3. Financial Difficulties: Loss of employment, unstable finances, debt, or poverty can all lead to economic adversity. These difficulties may cause a great deal of worry and uncertainty.

4. Relationship Problems: Whether in families, friendships, or romantic relationships, tension or breakup can lead to adversity. Divorces, separations, and conflicts can all cause emotional upheaval.

5. Environmental Factors: Adversity related to the environment includes problems relating to climate change, natural disasters, and other ecological or environmental issues that have an impact on both communities and individuals.

6. Personal Loss and Grief: Losing a loved one due to their passing away or separation can be extremely difficult. Bereavement and grief are normal reactions to these types of hardship.

7. Workplace Challenges: Unhappiness with one's job, disagreements with coworkers, losing one's job, or experiencing setbacks in one's career can all lead to workplace adversity. Burnout and stress are frequent results of problems at work.

8. Educational Barriers: Learners may encounter challenges related to access to high-quality education, learning disabilities, or academic difficulties.

9. Cultural and Societal Factors: Systemic injustices, discrimination, and other cultural and societal issues can all have an impact on adversity. For both individuals and communities, these elements may provide difficulties and obstacles.

10. Personal Decisions and Errors: Personal decisions and errors can lead to some adversity. It's critical to understand that hardship can also lead to growth and important life lessons.

11. Historical and Global Events: Adversity is not limited to personal experiences; it can also encompass worldwide occurrences that affect entire communities, such as pandemics, political upheavals, and economic downturns.

12. Aging and Life Stages: Adversity takes the form of aging-related challenges like physical decline or loss of independence. Every stage of life has its own distinct set of difficulties.

Knowing the causes of adversity is crucial because it makes it possible for us to build coping mechanisms and empathy for others. Adversity is a common experience for all people, and overcoming it frequently allows people to find their inner resilience and strength.

Difficulties and mishaps.

Difficulties and mishaps are inherent pieces of the human experience. They envelop an expansive scope of troubles and obstructions that people experience throughout their lives. Understanding difficulties and mishaps is fundamental for versatility and self-awareness. Here are key parts of difficulties and mishaps:

- **Variety of Encounters:** Difficulties and mishaps come in different structures, including individual, proficient, close to home, and actual difficulties. They can be minor burdens or significant life-changing occasions.

- **Unforeseen Nature:** Difficulties and mishaps frequently emerge suddenly, upsetting the ordinary course of life. These startling occasions can test a singular's versatility and strength.

- **Learning and Valuable learning experiences:** While difficulties can be troublesome, they additionally present open doors for learning and self-improvement. Beating affliction can prompt the securing of new abilities, expanded mindfulness, and improved strength.

- **Profound Effect:** Difficulties and mishaps can summon a scope of feelings, including disappointment, stress, misery, and once in a while despair. Recognizing and dealing with these feelings is a fundamental piece of adapting.

- **Critical thinking:** Confronting difficulties and misfortunes frequently includes critical thinking. People should examine what is happening, distinguish possible arrangements, and make a move to resolve the issue.

- **Constancy:** Defeating difficulties and mishaps regularly requires tirelessness and assurance. It might include various endeavors and a guarantee to push through difficulty.

- **Survival methods:** Creating successful ways of dealing with stress is imperative for overseeing difficulties and mishaps. These procedures might incorporate looking for help from companions or experts, rehearsing taking care of oneself, and using pressure-decrease strategies.

- **Versatility and Transformation:** Effectively exploring difficulties and mishaps can upgrade a singular's resilience and their capacity to adjust to future challenges. It can likewise support fearlessness in one's ability to beat difficulty.

- **Encouraging group of people:** areas of strength for an organization, involving companions, family, guides, or instructors, can give support and help during testing times.

- **Reflection and Development:** Difficulties and mishaps can prompt self-awareness and self-revelation. Considering one's encounters and illustrations learned can be a groundbreaking cycle.

- **Difficult exercise:** Finding some kind of harmony between dealing with difficulties directly and perceiving when to look for help or make a stride back is fundamental. It's not generally important to face difficulty alone.

- **Long-haul Point of view:** While quick difficulties might be upsetting, keeping a drawn-out point of view can assist people with maintaining their emphasis on their bigger life objectives and yearnings.

Understanding the idea of moves and mishaps can engage people to foster powerful methodologies for adapting and flourishing notwithstanding misfortune. It's critical to recognize that everybody experiences hardships in their lives, and these difficulties can be instrumental in cultivating self-improvement and strength.

Adapting to Challenges.

Adapting to challenges is fundamental expertise that permits people to explore testing circumstances and keep up with their prosperity. Survival techniques can differ contingent upon the idea of the trouble, yet here are a few general standards for really adapting to challenges:

1. Recognize Your Feelings: Perceive and approve your sentiments. It's OK to encounter a scope of feelings when confronted with troubles. Recognizing and tolerating your feelings is the most vital phase in adapting.

2. Look for Help: Feel free to connect with companions, family, or a specialist for basic encouragement. Conversing with somebody you trust can give solace and viewpoint.

3. Critical thinking: For viable hardships, use critical thinking techniques. Separate the issue into more modest, reasonable advances, and think about expected arrangements. This proactive methodology can assist you with recapturing a feeling of control.

4. Taking care of oneself: Focus on taking care of oneself, including keeping a solid daily schedule. Workouts, appropriate sustenance, and sufficient rest are significant for physical and close-to-home prosperity.

5. Care and Unwinding: Care methods, like contemplation and profound breathing, can assist you with remaining grounded and lessening pressure. These practices advance unwinding and a feeling of quiet.

6. Limit Negative Self-Talk: Challenge and reevaluate negative contemplations. Supplant self-analysis with self-sympathy. Positive self-talk can help your strength.

7. Put forth Sensible Objectives: If the trouble includes a drawn-out objective, separate it into more modest, reachable objectives. This gradual advancement can inspire and enable you.

8. Maintain Point of view: Challenges frequently feel overpowering at the time. Attempt to keep a more extensive point of view and advise yourself that difficulties are a piece of life, yet they don't characterize you as long as you can remember.

9. Gain from Difficulty: View hardships as any open doors for self-awareness and learning. Consider what you can acquire from the experience and how it can make you more grounded.

10. Develop Flexibility: Strength is the capacity to return quickly from affliction. Develop this quality by creating adapting abilities, a positive outlook, and faith in your capacity to defeat challenges.

11. Time and Tolerance: Comprehend that adapting to challenges might take time. Show restraint toward yourself and permit yourself the space to recuperate and recuperate.

12. Look for Proficient Assistance: If the trouble is especially difficult or causing serious pain, think about looking for help with psychological well-being proficiency. They can give direction and remedial mediation.

13. Rest on Your Encouraging Group of People: Talk about your thoughts and hardships with your encouraging group of people. You don't need to go through testing times alone, and your friends and family can offer direction and solace.

Adapting to hardships is a unique cycle that might include a blend of these procedures. The key is to fit your way to deal with the particular test and your singular requirements. Building areas of strength for and adapting abilities can engage you to explore life's promising and less promising times with versatility and beauty.

Defeating Life's Hindrances.

Defeating life's hindrance is much the same as leaving on a great experience loaded up with unanticipated difficulties and potential open doors for self-improvement. To explore this excursion, you should develop a mentality that sees hindrances as venturing stones as opposed to barriers. An uplifting perspective and a hopeful standpoint are your sidekicks on this journey, permitting you to change misfortune into an impetus for change.

At the start of any excursion, having an unmistakable objective as a top priority is fundamental. Laying out obvious objectives gives guidance and motivation, directing you away from capricious floating and towards substantial accomplishments. These objectives become your directing stars, spurring you to push forward when confronted with affliction.

As you progress, you experience hindrances that might appear to be inconceivable. This is where your critical thinking abilities become possibly the most important factor. Every hindrance is a riddle to be disentangled, requesting scientific reasoning and innovative investigation of likely arrangements. You separate complex difficulties into sensible advances, similar to a carefully prepared pioneer outlining a course through an unknown region.

Versatility is the imperceptible defensive layer that safeguards you from the blows of difficulty. It's anything but a proper quality yet an expertise that you can sharpen after some time. Resilience is the craft of quickly returning, a quality that empowers you to adjust and endure in any event, when the way appears to be deceptive. It's the conviction that you can face any hardship and arise more grounded on the opposite side.

On this excursion, you are in good company. Look for help from individuals who have crossed comparative landscapes, be they companions, family, coaches, or experts. They are your kindred voyagers, offering direction, consolation, and different points of view that can reveal insight into the most obscure of ways.

Hindrance frequently require variation. Life is unusual, and adaptability is your compass when the course changes suddenly. Embrace change as a potential chance to develop and reclassify your methodology.

While investigating, be caring to yourself. Self-sympathy is a delicate hand on your shoulder during testing times, an update that it's OK to waver and stagger. Self-empathy replaces self-analysis with understanding, guaranteeing that you are your most confided-in partner.

Steadiness is the light that lights your direction through the haziest of evenings. It's the obligation to continue to push ahead, in any event, when progress is slow, and misfortunes appear to be difficult. It's the unfaltering conviction that each step carries you nearer to your objective.

Difficulties become venturing stones whenever you view them as any open doors for development. Each stagger is an example, an opportunity to investigate what turned out badly, change your methodology, and arise smarter and stronger.

Compelling close-to-home guideline assists you with staying cool-headed amid the whirlwind of feelings that snags can set off. Procedures like profound breathing, care, and contemplation act as your anchor, offering a feeling of quiet and control.

Using time productively guarantees that you proficiently distribute your assets, in any event, while the ticking clock seems like your foe. Focus on errands and use time usage procedures to remain coordinated and on target.

Self-adequacy is the faith in your capacities. It's the resolute conviction that you have the stuff to overcome any obstruction. Building self-viability resembles manufacturing a strong blade; it's your weapon against misfortune.

Praise every triumph, regardless of how little, as you venture ahead. Perceiving your accomplishments, regardless of how minor, energizes your inspiration and builds up your faith in your capacity to defeat impediments.

Move toward challenges with an arrangements-situated outlook. Center around finding answers instead of harping on issues, and you'll wind up progressing with reason and clearness.

Keep a drawn-out viewpoint. Recollect that the deterrents you face are transient, fleeting disturbances in the great embroidery of your life's process. This more extensive view reduces the prompt weight.

Your encouraging group of people is a gold mine of intelligence and consolation. Draw on the strength and experiences of companions, family, coaches, and care groups when you want direction and consolation.

In situations where impediments seem unfavorable or influence your psychological well-being, looking for proficient direction from advisors, guides, or mentors is a demonstration of taking care of oneself and shrewdness. These specialists give the guides and devices to explore even the most slippery territory.

Finally, support yourself by taking care of yourself. Focus on exercises that advance unwinding, rest, and bliss, for they are the desert springs of rest on your challenging excursion.

Embrace these standards and techniques as your partners on your journey through life's obstructions. Challenges are not impossible; they are the cauldron where your personality is fashioned and your resilience is sharpened. You are the gutsy wayfarer of your own story, and it is through your excursion that you find the full degree of your solidarity and potential.

CHAPTER 3

Building a Resilient Mindset.

Resilience is the capacity to return from misfortune, and expertise can be developed and fortified over the long haul. Building a versatile outlook resembles strengthening the underpinning of a house; it empowers you to face life's hardships and arise more grounded. This is the way to foster a strong outlook:

1. Uplifting perspective: Start by embracing an inspirational perspective on life. Consider difficulties to be valuable open doors for development, not as unfavorable deterrents. Hopefulness is the foundation of flexibility.

2. **Mindfulness:** Figure out your close-to-home reactions to affliction. Perceive your sentiments and recognize them without judgment. This mindfulness is the most vital phase in dealing with your feelings.

3. Critical thinking Abilities: Foster solid critical thinking abilities. Separate complex issues into reasonable advances, investigate expected arrangements and make a move. This proactive methodology enables you to explore challenges.

4. Versatility: Embrace change and be versatile. Life is loaded with unforeseen turns, and the capacity to change your arrangements and techniques is crucial despite affliction.

5. Survival techniques: Construct a toolbox of compelling ways of dealing with especially difficult times. This incorporates unwinding strategies, care practices, and stress-decrease techniques that assist you with remaining formed in tough spots.

6. Tirelessness: Develop diligence. Comprehend that misfortunes are essential for the excursion, yet they don't characterize your whole story. Continue to push ahead, in any event, when the street is testing.

7. Gain as a matter of fact: Each trouble contains important examples. Use difficulties as any open doors for self-improvement and personal development. Ponder what you've realized and how it can make you stronger.

8. Social Help: Sustain your encouraging group of people. Companions, family, coaches, and care groups give profound food and direction. Rest on them when you want consolation and viewpoint.

9. Profound Guideline: Expert close-to-home guideline. Practice profound breathing, reflection, and care to oversee pressure and tension. These methods advance a feeling of quiet and control.

10. Using time effectively: Productively deal with your time and assets. Focus on assignments and put forth sensible objectives to forestall overpowering pressure.

11. Self-Adequacy: Fortify your faith in your capacities. Trust in your ability to beat difficulties is a strong inspiration. Set little, feasible objectives to fabricate self-viability.

12. Observe Progress: Recognize and praise your triumphs, regardless of how minor. Perceiving your accomplishments helps your inspiration and builds up your faith in your versatility.

13. Arrangements Situated Concentration: Focus on finding arrangements instead of harping on issues. An arrangements-situated mentality assists you in approaching hardships with clearness and reason.

14. Long haul Point of view: Keep a more extensive point of view. Hindrances are transitory; they don't characterize your life's aggregate. Remember your definitive objectives to lighten prompt weights.

15. Proficient Direction: Look for proficient assistance when difficulties are uncommonly troublesome or influencing your emotional well-being. Specialists, instructors, or mentors can give master direction and restorative mediation.

16. Taking care of oneself: Focus on taking care of oneself, guaranteeing you set aside a few minutes for unwinding, rest, and exercises that give you pleasure. Taking care of oneself keeps you truly and intellectually versatile.

Building a strong outlook is a continuous interaction. It's tied in with fostering the psychological and profound solidarity to confront affliction with certainty and versatility. With these systems, you can sustain your versatility, permitting you to flourish notwithstanding life's difficulties.

Positive Thinking and Growth Mindset.

Positive reasoning and a development mentality are two useful assets for self-awareness and versatility. The two of them add to a strong mentality by encouraging good faith, versatility, and a proactive way to deal with difficulties. This is the way they work and how you can develop them:

1. Positive Reasoning:

Positive reasoning includes keeping a hopeful and confident standpoint. It doesn't mean overlooking or denying issues; all things being equal, it's tied in with moving toward challenges with a valuable disposition. This is the way to cultivate positive reasoning:

- Practice Appreciation: Consistently offer thanks for the positive parts of your life. Zeroing in on what you have as opposed to what you need can help your general standpoint.

- Challenge Negative Contemplations: Become mindful of negative self-talk and effectively challenge it. Supplant self-analysis with self-empathy and productive, empowering considerations.

- Encircle Yourself with Inspiration: Invest energy with individuals who elevate and uphold you. Positive social associations can significantly affect your mentality.

- **Put forth Reasonable Objectives:** Set feasible, explicit objectives for yourself. The outcome of accomplishing these objectives can support your uplifting perspective.

- **Care and Reflection:** Practice care and contemplation to remain present at the time and lessen pressure. These methods can assist you with keeping an inspirational outlook.

- **Perception:** Imagine your ideal results and achievement. This can give you a feeling of confidence and spur you to pursue your objectives.

2. Development Mentality:

A development mentality is a conviction that capacities and insight can be created through devotion and difficult work. It empowers an affection for learning and a readiness to embrace difficulties. This is the way to develop a development outlook:

- **Embrace Difficulties:** Welcome difficulties as any open doors for development. Instead of staying away from challenges, consider them to be opportunities to learn and get to the next level.

- Gain from Disappointment: Don't fear disappointment; see it as a venturing stone to progress. Investigate what turned out badly, make changes, and utilize the experience for your potential benefit.

- Exertion and Determination: Perceive that work and diligence are key elements in accomplishing your objectives. In any event, when confronted with mishaps, keep major areas of strength for an ethic and continue.

- Consider Analysis to be Input: Criticism, in any event, when basic, can be an important wellspring of learning and improvement. Embrace useful analysis as a method for developing.

- Remain Inquisitive: Develop a characteristic interest in the planet. Be available to groundbreaking thoughts, viewpoints, and encounters. This receptiveness to learning is a sign of a development outlook.

- Trust in Your Capacity to Change: Comprehend that your capacities and characteristics are not fixed. You can change, adjust, and foster in different aspects of your life.

- Observe Exertion and Progress: Shift your concentration from just commending results to praising the work you put in and the headway you make en route.

By joining positive reasoning and a development outlook, you foster a versatile way to deal with life's difficulties. You keep a hopeful viewpoint, having faith in your ability to learn, adjust, and flourish. This encourages strength as well as advances self-awareness and a feeling of satisfaction in your excursion.

Self-Compassion.

Self-Compassion: A Key to Strength and Prosperity

Self-compassion is a strong and extraordinary quality that assumes an imperative part in building versatility and advancing by and large prosperity. It includes treating oneself with a similar consideration, understanding, and backing that we would propose to a dear companion. This is the way self-sympathy adds to resilience and moves toward developing it:

<u>**Why Self-Compassion Matters:**</u>

1. Profound Guideline: Self-compassion directs your feelings, particularly during testing times. It permits you to recognize troublesome feelings without judgment, prompting more prominent close-to-home steadiness.

2. Diminished Self-Analysis: By supplanting self-analysis with Self-Compassion, you make a better internal discourse. This shift encourages self-acknowledgment and confidence.

3. Improved Versatility: Self-compassion is firmly connected to flexibility. It gives the close-to-home strength and confidence expected to confront affliction with more prominent versatility and self-control.

4. More prominent Inspiration: Oddly, Self-Compassion frequently prompts more prominent inspiration for personal growth. At the point when you treat yourself with thoughtfulness, you're bound to make valuable moves to address difficulties.

Developing Self-Compassion:

1. Care: Begin by turning out to be more aware of your viewpoints and self-talk. Notice when self-analysis or negative contemplations emerge. Care makes mindfulness, which is the most vital phase in rolling out an improvement.

2. Practice Self-Thoughtfulness: Indulge yourself with the very graciousness and care that you would offer a dear companion. When confronted with challenges, ask yourself, "What might I tell a companion in this present circumstance?" Then, at that point, stretch out a similar sympathy to yourself.

3. Embrace Blemish: Comprehend that flaw is a piece of the human experience. It's alright to commit errors and have imperfections. Acknowledge yourself with every one of your blemishes.

4. Perceive Normal Mankind: Understand that everybody faces difficulties and hardships throughout everyday life. You're in good company in your battles. Recognizing our common humankind can diminish sensations of separation.

5. Self-Compassion Breaks: Utilize self-sympathy breaks, which are short, careful activities. At the point when you face a predicament, pause for a minute to recognize your misery, advise yourself that enduring is a piece of life, and deal yourself graciousness.

6. Look for Help: Feel free to help from companions, family, or experts. They can give direction and consolation, which supplements your Self-Compassion endeavors.

7. Pardoning: Excuse yourself for previous oversights and let go of self-fault. Clutching feelings of spite, particularly against yourself, can prevent your capacity to push ahead.

8. Taking care of oneself: Focus on taking care of oneself practices that feed your physical and profound prosperity.

Participate in exercises that give you pleasure and unwinding.

9. Self-Compassion Journaling: Keep a diary where you compose self-empathetic proclamations to yourself. This can be an incredible asset to support Self-Compassion and counter self-analysis.

By developing self-sympathy, you can fabricate major areas of strength for resilience and prosperity. It engages you to confront difficulty with benevolence and confidence, at last empowering you to flourish despite life's difficulties. Self-compassion is certainly not an indication of shortcomings however a demonstration of your solidarity and mindfulness.

<u>Emotional Intelligence</u>

The capacity to understand anyone on a deeper level: The Way to Versatility and Achievement

The capacity to understand people on a profound level (EI) is a fundamental quality that adds to both individual versatility and outcomes in different parts of life. It alludes to the capacity to perceive, comprehend, make due, and successfully utilize your feelings and the feelings of others. This is the way the capacity to understand people on a deeper level is fundamental for resilience and moves toward improving it:

Why The ability to understand anyone on a profound level Matters:

1. Mindfulness: The ability to understand people on a profound level starts with mindfulness. Figuring out your feelings, triggers, and responses permits you to explore difficulties with more noteworthy understanding and control.

2. Feeling Guideline: Sincerely keen people can deal with their feelings successfully. They don't allow gloomy feelings to overpower them, which is an essential expertise for strength.

3. Compassion: Sympathy, a central part of the capacity to understand individuals on a deeper level, helps you comprehend and interface with others. It cultivates positive connections, fundamental for individual help and achievement.

4. Relational Abilities: A high capacity to appreciate anyone on a profound level converts areas of strength into abilities. This is crucial for building and keeping up with connections, whether in private or expert life.

Developing Ability to appreciate people at their core:

1. Mindfulness: Begin by creating mindfulness. Consistently think about your feelings, their causes, and their effect on your viewpoints and activities. Journaling can be a useful practice.

2. Feeling Guideline: Figure out how to deal with your feelings, particularly in testing circumstances. Methods like profound breathing, care, and contemplation can help with feeling guidelines.

3. Compassion: Practice undivided attention and attempt to see circumstances according to others' points of view. Creating compassion includes understanding and valuing the feelings of people around you.

4. Interactive abilities: Fortify your interactive abilities by building positive connections and successful correspondence. Participate in transparent discoursed, look for criticism, and show veritable interest in others.

5. Compromise: Foster compromise abilities, which are fundamental for overseeing conflicts and false impressions helpfully. Keeping away from pointless contentions can preserve profound energy.

6. Stress The board: Sincerely shrewd people are gifted at overseeing pressure. Focus on taking care of oneself practices, like ordinary activity, appropriate sustenance, and adequate rest.

7. Inspirational perspective: Develop an inspirational perspective on life. Idealism and strength frequently remain closely connected. Center around arrangements as opposed to harping on issues.

8. Care: Care practices can increment the capacity to appreciate anyone on a profound level by assisting you with remaining present, focused, and mindful of your feelings at the time.

9. Constant Learning: Embrace a development mentality. Perceiving that capacity to understand individuals at their core is an expertise that can be created and worked on over the long run. Continue learning and looking for ways of upgrading your EI.

10. Look for Input: Effectively look for criticism from confided-in companions, coaches, or associates. Their experiences can give important points of view on your ability to understand individuals on a deeper level and regions for development.

Improving the capacity to understand people on a profound level is a continuous excursion, and it assumes a critical part in private strength and generally speaking achievement. By getting it and dealing with your feelings, understanding others, and building solid relational abilities, you explore difficulties all the more successfully as well as cultivate good connections and set out open doors for development and satisfaction in your own proficient life.

CHAPTER 4

Nurturing Physical Resilience: Building a Strong Foundation for Life

Physical Adaptability is the capability of your body to repel, acclimatize to, and recover from colorful physical stressors and challenges. It's a foundation of overall adaptability and well-being. Then are ways to nurture physical adaptability

1. Regular Exercise:

- Engage in regular physical exertion that includes a combination of cardiovascular, strength, and resilience exercises.

- Exercise helps make physical strength, abidance, and cardiovascular health, which are crucial factors of adaptability.

2. Acceptable Rest:

- Prioritize getting sufficient sleep each night(generally 7- 9 hours for grown-ups) to allow your body to recover and rejuvenate.

- Quality sleep enhances cognitive function, emotional stability, and physical recovery.

3. Balanced Nutrition:

- Maintain a balanced and nutritional diet rich in fruits, vegetables, whole grains, spare proteins, and healthy fats.

- Proper nutrition provides the essential nutrients your body needs for energy, growth, and recovery.

4. Stress operation:

- Practice stress-reduction ways, similar to contemplation, deep breathing, and relaxation exercises.

- Habitual stress can weaken the body's adaptability, so managing stress is vital for physical well-being.

5. Hydration:
- Remain sufficiently doused by drinking sufficient water over the day.
- Proper hydration is essential for maintaining overall health and adaptability.

6. Injury Prevention:
- Be aware of your physical safety to avoid gratuitous injuries. Use proper form and outfit when exercising or engaging in physical conditioning.

7. Regular Health Check- ups:
- Schedule regular check-ups with healthcare professionals to cover your overall health and describe any implicit issues beforehand.

8. make a probative terrain:
   - compass yourself with a probative social network and a terrain that promotes physical well-being.

9. Recovery Days:
   - Incorporate rest and recovery days into your fitness routine to allow your body to heal and help overtraining.

10. Rigidity:
   - Be adaptable in your physical conditioning. Modify your routines as demanded to accommodate injuries, age, or other changing circumstances.

11. Mental Health:
   - Fete the profound connection between physical and internal health. Prioritize your

internal well-being as it directly impacts your physical adaptability.

Nurturing physical adaptability not only prepares your body to handle physical challenges but also contributes to emotional and internal adaptability. A healthy body is better equipped to manage with stress, recover from illness, and maintain a positive outlook on life. It forms the foundation for overall well-being and the capability to thrive in the face of life's challenges.

The Role of Exercise and Nutrition in Building Physical Resilience.

Exercise and nourishment are foundations of actual strength, assuming vital parts in setting up your body to endure and adjust to different actual stressors. Here is a more intensive glance at their importance and how they add to building actual flexibility:

1. Work out:

Customary actual work offers a heap of advantages that straightforwardly improve actual flexibility:

- **Strength and Perseverance:** Exercise, especially strength preparation and cardiovascular exercises, assists in developing muscle fortitude and perseverance. A solid body is better prepared to deal with actual difficulties and recuperate all the more proficiently.

- **Cardiovascular Wellbeing:** Cardiovascular activities, like running, swimming, or cycling, work on your heart and lung well-being. A vigorous cardiovascular framework improves your body's capacity to convey oxygen and supplements to tissues, supporting general flexibility.

- **Bone Wellbeing:** Weight-bearing activities, such as strolling and weightlifting, help keep up with and work on bone thickness. Solid bones are less vulnerable to cracks, which is fundamental for flexibility, particularly as you age.

- **Adaptability and Versatility:** Extending and adaptability practices work on your scope of movement and joint adaptability. This lessens the gamble of wounds and improves your body's versatility.

- **Stress Decrease:** Exercise is a characteristic pressure minimizer. Actual work discharges endorphins, which can reduce pressure and upgrade your psychological flexibility.

- Safe Capability: Ordinary activity can support your insusceptible framework, making your body stronger against contaminations and sicknesses.

- Mental Versatility: Exercise significantly affects psychological wellness. It can mitigate side effects of uneasiness and melancholy, upgrade mental capability, and work on profound prosperity, which, thus, adds to generally speaking versatility.

2. Nourishment:

Appropriate sustenance is the fuel that controls your body and contributes fundamentally to actual flexibility:

- Energy and Recuperation: A reasonable eating regimen gives the energy your body needs for everyday exercises and recuperation. Supplement thick food varieties guarantee that your body has the assets to fix itself after actual pressure.

- Muscle Support: Sufficient protein admission is fundamental for muscle upkeep and development. Protein fixes and assembles muscle tissue, adding to actual strength.

- Bone Wellbeing: Calcium and vitamin D, frequently obtained through dairy items, salad greens, and daylight openness, are critical for bone well-being and crack avoidance.

- Invulnerable Capability: Nutrients and minerals, like L-ascorbic acid, vitamin D, and zinc, support your safe framework, making your body stronger against sicknesses.

- Hydration: Remaining enough hydrated is crucial for general well-being and versatility. Appropriate hydration upholds actual execution, mental capability, and temperature guidelines.

- Stomach Wellbeing: A sound stomach microbiome, upheld by an eating regimen wealthy in fiber and probiotics, significantly affects the resistant framework and generally speaking wellbeing.

- Cerebrum Wellbeing: Supplements like omega-3 unsaturated fats, tracked down in greasy fish and nuts, are fundamental for mind well-being and mental capability.

- Mindset and Mental Flexibility: Nourishment can influence temperament and mental versatility. Eats less carbs wealthy in entire food varieties, like organic products, vegetables, and entire grains, are related to better mental prosperity.

In synopsis, exercise and nourishment are necessary to build actual flexibility. Normal active work improves strength, perseverance, and flexibility, while legitimate nourishment gives the energy and supplements your body needs for recuperation and in general prosperity. When consolidated, they make major areas of strength for actual versatility that reaches out to mental and profound resilience too.

Rest and Recovery: The Essential Elements of Physical and Mental Resilience.

Rest and recovery are frequently misjudged yet are basic parts of both physical and mental strength. They are the periods during which your body and brain recuperate, adjust, and get ready for future difficulties. Here's the reason rest and recuperation are fundamental and how to integrate them into your life:

Actual Strength:

1. Muscle Recuperation: After practice or actual effort, your muscles need time to recuperate. Rest permits them to fix and develop further, adding to actual versatility.

2. Injury Counteraction: Sufficient rest forestalls abuse wounds and permits minor wounds to mend. Pushing through agony can prompt more critical issues and thwart versatility.

3. Energy Reclamation: Rest recharges your energy levels, both truly and intellectually. It guarantees that you have the essentialness expected to confront life's difficulties.

4. Chemical Equilibrium: Quality rest and rest add to hormonal equilibrium, which influences different parts of actual well-being, including muscle development and general prosperity.

5. Safe Capability: Rest is fundamental for a hearty resistant framework. Rest, specifically, upholds your body's capacity to fend off diseases and ailments.

Mental Versatility:

1. Stress Decrease: Rest and unwinding are essential for diminishing pressure. Persistent pressure can debilitate mental flexibility, making it vital to integrate times of unwinding into your daily practice.

2. Profound Prosperity: Mental resilience is intently attached to close-to-home prosperity. Satisfactory rest keeps up with stable temperaments and forestalls close-to-home weariness.

3. Mental Capability: Rest is fundamental for mental capability. It upgrades memory solidification, critical abilities to think, and innovative reasoning, all of which add to mental strength.

4. Mental Strength: Rest permits you to process and recuperate from sincerely testing encounters, expanding mental flexibility.

Instructions to Consolidate Rest and Recuperation:

1. Quality Rest: Focus on getting sufficient quality rest. Hold back nothing long stretches of rest each night for grown-ups, as lack of rest can impede physical and mental strength.

2. Dynamic Recuperation: Take part in dynamic recuperation, like delicate activity, yoga, or extending, on rest days. This can assist with muscle recuperation and adaptability.

3. Care and Unwinding: Practice care, reflection, or profound breathing activities to advance unwinding and decrease pressure.

4. Lay out Limits: Put down stopping points to guarantee you possess energy for rest and recuperation. Stay away from overcommitting or exhausting, as it can prompt burnout.

5. Turn off: Disengage from screens and innovation, particularly before sleep time. This advances better rest quality and mental rest.

6. Social Association: Invest energy with companions friends and family to unwind and appreciate social help, which is crucial for mental flexibility.

7. Side interests and Happiness: Take part in side interests and exercises that give you pleasure and unwinding. Adjusting work and recreation upholds mental strength.

8. Sustenance: Keep a fair eating regimen to furnish your body and psyche with vital supplements for recuperation and flexibility.

Recall that rest and recovery are not indications of shortcomings but rather are fundamental for building physical and mental versatility. They are periods during which your body and brain reconstruct and plan to confront future difficulties. Integrating rest into your routine is an interest in your general prosperity and your capacity to flourish even with life's requests.

Stress Management: Nurturing Resilience in the Face of Life's Challenges.

Important pressure on the board is a major part of the structure and keeping up with inflexibility. It furnishes you with the accouterments to acclimatize to and acclimate to the requests and pressures of life. They are methodologies and strategies to help you with overseeing pressure and support your versatility:

1. Distinguish Stressors: Begin by distinguishing the wellsprings of stress in your life. Perceiving unequivocal stressors is the most vital phase in overseeing them.

2. Care and Contemplation: Practice care and reflection to remain present at the time and dwindle pressure. These styles can help you stay cool and centered.

3. Profound Relaxing: Profound breathing conditioning can fleetly quiet your body's pressure response. At the point when you feel upset, take a couple of full breaths to decompress and pull together.

4. Normal Active work: Share in normal exertion. Active work works on your factual good as well as delivers endorphins that help your disposition and dwindle pressure.

5. Smart overeating: Keep a decent eating routine. licit aliment gives your body the energy and supplements it must to acclimatize to pressure.

6. Satisfactory Rest: Focus on rest. The absence of rest can fuel pressure and frustrate strength. Go for the gold long stretches of value rest each evening.

7. Using time effectively: Feasible that using time productively can drop the sensation of being overpowered. Focus on undertakings, put forth practical objects, and try not to over-burden your schedule.

8. Social Help: Rest in your encouraging group of people. Companions and musketeers and family can offer profound help and a harkening observance during testing times.

9. Put down Stopping points: Put down clear stopping points to keep a solid balance between serious and delightful conditioning. Stay down from overcommitting and enjoy reprieves when needed.

10. Stress-drop Exercises: Take part in exercises you appreciate and view as unwinding. Side interests, nature rambles, and inventive hobbies can be successful pressure minimizers.

11. Positive logic: Develop an uplifting perspective on life. Center around arrangements rather than issues, and practice appreciation to help your inflexibility.

12. Look for complete backing: Feel free to complete directions when needed. Specialists, counselors, and instructors can offer master help for overseeing pressure.

13. Near-to-home Guideline: Foster near-to-home guideline capacities to oversee extraordinary passions. styles like tone-easing, establishing conditioning, and tone-sympathy can be useful.

14. Concession: Ameliorate your concession capacities to oversee relational pressure. Compelling correspondence and concession can fortify connections and inflexibility.

15. Ideal Setting: Put forth accessible objects and break them into further modest, sensible advances. Achieving these objectives can help your certainty and lessen pressure.

16. Streamline and Clean up: Clean up your physical and internal space. perfecting your life can dwindle pressure and create a feeling of quiet.

Stress is a piece of life, but still important pressure on the board empowers you to explore difficulties no sweat. By integrating these systems into your everyday diurnal schedule, you can construct and support your versatility, guaranteeing that you are more set to defy the requests and pressures of life. Recollect that resilience is not the space of stress still the capacity to flourish despite it.

CHAPTER 5

Social Support and Connection: The Pillars of Resilience.

Social Support and Connection associations with others are fundamental for building and keeping up with versatility. Individuals are innately friendly animals, and these associations act as a security net during life's difficulties. Here's the reason social help and association are imperative for strength and ways of supporting them:

Why Social Support Matters:

1. **Basic encouragement:** Social associations offer profound help, offering solace and understanding during troublesome

times. Discussing your thoughts and encounters with others can ease pressure and encourage close-to-home strength.

2. Critical thinking: Believed companions friends and family can offer different points of view and answers for issues you could confront. Cooperative critical thinking upgrades your strength by giving you a more extensive scope of systems to address difficulties.

3. Stress Decrease: Drawing in with others can be a wellspring of unwinding and stress decrease. Investing energy with companions, family, or care groups can reduce pressure and advance close-to-home prosperity.

4. Approval: Social associations give approval and a feeling of having a place. Feeling accepted and acknowledged by others adds to your identity worth and versatility.

5. Adapting Assets: Your encouraging group of people can act as an important asset for adapting to misfortune. Whether it's a listening ear, reasonable help, or direction, these assets upgrade your capacity to defeat difficulties.

Sustaining Social Support and Connection:

1. Keep up with Connections: Put time and exertion into sustaining existing connections. Keep in contact with loved ones, and try to fortify those associations.

2. Convey Transparently: Encourage transparent correspondence in your connections. Share your contemplations, sentiments, and encounters with those you trust.

3. Offer Help: offer help to others in your organization. Thoughtful gestures and help can fortify your associations and construct correspondence.

4. Join Gatherings: Take part in friendly exercises and join bunches that line up with your inclinations and values. This is an incredible method for meeting similar people and extending your informal organization.

5. Look for Proficient Assistance: On the off chance that you're managing complex intense subject matters or battling to track down friendly help, think about looking for help from a specialist, instructor, or care group.

6. Offer Thanks: Show appreciation for individuals in your day-to-day existence. Offering thanks can extend your associations and make a positive, steady climate.

7. Higher expectations without compromise: Spotlight on the nature of your connections instead of the amount. Significant, profound associations essentially affect your flexibility.

8. Put down Stopping points: Lay out sound limits in your connections to keep harmony between your prosperity and supporting others.

9. Online People group: Consider joining the web networks or care groups if in-person associations are restricted. These stages can offer significant help and associations.

10. Volunteer: Chipping in can assist you with building associations while rewarding the local area. It's a method for encountering the advantages of social help while likewise adding to the strength of others.

11. Undivided attention: Practice undivided attention in your communications with others. Be completely present and mindful of what they are talking about, making a more profound association.

Recall that social support and connection are not indications of shortcomings but rather are wellsprings of solidarity and strength. Fabricating and keeping up with these connections make a powerful establishment to assist you with flourishing notwithstanding life's difficulties. Connecting and interfacing with others can give solace, arrangements, and a feeling of having a place, all of which add to your versatility.

The Importance of Relationships: Building Blocks of Resilience and Well-Being.

Relationships are key structure blocks of versatility and prosperity. They assume an essential part in your capacity to adapt to life's difficulties and flourish even with misfortune. Here's the reason connections are of foremost significance and how they add to versatility:

1. Basic encouragement:

- Connections offer close-to-home help, which is priceless during troublesome times. Believed companions, friends and family offer solace, understanding, and a place of refuge to communicate your sentiments and fears.

2. Feeling of Having a Place:

- Significant connections make a feeling of having a place and connectedness. Feeling a piece of a local area or organization improves your confidence and supports your feeling of character.

3. Critical thinking:

- Social associations offer a different scope of points of view and answers for issues. Cooperative critical thinking reinforces your versatility by giving a more extensive arrangement of methodologies to address difficulties.

4. Stress Decrease:

- Drawing in with others can be a wellspring of unwinding and stress decrease. Investing energy with companions, family, or care groups can lighten pressure and advance profound prosperity.

5. Approval and Acknowledgment:

- Social associations give approval and a feeling of acknowledgment. Feeling accepted and acknowledged by others adds to your healthy identity worth and strength.

6. Adapting Assets:

- Your encouraging group of people fills in as an important asset for adapting to difficulty. Whether it's a listening ear, reasonable help, or direction, these assets upgrade your capacity to conquer difficulties.

7. Observing Victories:

- Positive connections give a stage to commending victories, both of all shapes and sizes. Imparting accomplishments to others supports your inspiration and builds up your faith in your flexibility.

8. Adapting to Misfortune:

- Connections likewise assume a critical part in assisting you with adapting to misfortune, despondency, and life changes. The help and comprehension of others can be a lifesaver during these difficult periods.

Sustaining and Fortifying Connections:

1. Correspondence: Encourage transparent correspondence in your connections. Share your considerations, sentiments, and encounters with those you trust.

2. Sympathy: Practice compassion by effectively tuning in and figuring out the feelings and viewpoints of others. Sympathetic associations develop your connections and strength.

3. Quality Time: Try to invest quality energy with friends and family. Taking part in significant exercises and discussions fortifies your bonds.

4. Compromise: Foster compromise abilities to valuably oversee relational issues. Compelling correspondence upgrades connections and flexibility.

5. Correspondence: offer help to others in your organization. Thoughtful gestures and help can reinforce your associations and assemble correspondence.

6. Limits: Lay out solid limits in your connections to keep harmony between your prosperity and supporting others.

7. Keep up with Connections: Put time and exertion into sustaining existing connections. Keep in contact with loved ones, and try to fortify those associations.

8. Online People group: Consider joining the web networks or care groups if in-person associations are restricted. These stages can offer significant help and associations.

9. Proficient Assistance: Look for proficient direction while managing complex intense subject matters or while battling to track down friendly help.

10. Offer Thanks: Show appreciation for individuals in your day-to-day existence. Offering thanks extends your associations and makes a positive, strong climate.

The Relationships you develop are wellsprings of euphoria as well as fundamental parts of your resilience and general prosperity. Connecting and associating with others, keeping up with open correspondence, and cultivating compassion and backing make a powerful establishment that empowers you to flourish despite life's difficulties.

Building a Supportive Network: Strengthening Your Resilience Foundation.

A supportive network is a pivotal component of strength, giving a security net during life's difficulties and offering assets for development and prosperity. This is the way to construct and keep serious areas of strength for an organization:

1. Recognize Your Requirements:
- Start by recognizing your particular requirements for help. Consider what sorts of help (close to home, pragmatic, educational) you require.

2. Develop Existing Connections:
- Sustain the connections you as of now have. Put time and exertion into keeping up

with and reinforcing associations with loved ones.

3. Look for Similar People group:
- Draw in with networks and gatherings that share your inclinations and values. Normal interests can give a strong groundwork for building steady associations.

4. Volunteer and Offer in return:
- Chipping in is a brilliant method for building associations while rewarding the local area. It permits you to encounter the advantages of social help while additionally adding to the resilience of others.

5. Proficient Organizations:
- Fabricate and extend your expert organizations. Partners and coaches can offer help, and direction, and open doors for development.

6. Support Gatherings:

- Join support bunches pertinent to your difficulties or interests. These gatherings offer a space to interface with people confronting comparative circumstances.

7. Online People group:

- Investigate online networks and discussions connected with your interests and battles. They can give a stage to interfacing with similar people.

8. Relational abilities:

- Foster powerful relational abilities. Being an attentive person and communicating sympathy improves your capacity to fabricate and keep up with significant associations.

9. Limits:

- Lay out sound limits in your connections. Balance your prosperity with the help you give to other people.

10. Correspondence:

- Offer help to others in your organization. Thoughtful gestures and help can fortify your associations and construct correspondence.

11. Look for Proficient Assistance:

- Go ahead and proficient direction when required. Specialists, guides, or mentors can offer master help in building and keeping a steady organization.

12. Expand Your Organization:

- Fabricate a different organization that incorporates different kinds of help and associations. Various people might offer remarkable qualities and assets.

13. Offer Thanks:

- Show appreciation for individuals in your day-to-day existence. Offering thanks can develop your associations and make a positive, strong climate.

14. Consistency and Standard Contact:

- Reliably keep in touch with people in your organization. Normal correspondence and connection fortify connections over the long haul.

A supportive network is a repository of versatility, offering a feeling of having a place, everyday reassurance, and assets to handle life's difficulties. By effectively fabricating and supporting these associations, you make a vigorous starting point for flexibility, guaranteeing that you are better prepared to confront difficulty and flourish despite life's requests.

Coping as a Community: Fostering Collective Resilience.

Coping as a local area is a strong way to deal with building aggregate strength, where people back and inspire each other during testing times. This is the way networks can meet up to sustain strength:

1. Open Correspondence:

- Encourage transparent correspondence inside the local area. Urge people to share their considerations, sentiments, and concerns. Undivided attention and compassion make a place of refuge for discourse.

2. Encouraging groups of people:

- Make or fortify encouraging groups of people inside the local area. These organizations can give close-to-home, pragmatic, and social help to those out of luck.

3. Shared Help:

- Energize shared help and correspondence. Networks can arrange help for weak individuals, like the older, people with handicaps, or those confronting monetary challenges.

4. Versatility Instruction:

- Offer to school and prepare on resilience building. Give assets and studios on pressure the executives, survival methods, and emotional wellness mindfulness.

5. Psychological well-being Administrations:

- Elevate admittance to psychological well-being administrations. Networks can lay out associations with emotional wellness experts and give assets to those out of luck.

6. Emergency Reaction Plans:

- Foster emergency reaction plans for the local area. This incorporates debacle readiness, crisis correspondence, and emotionally supportive networks for people impacted by emergencies.

7. Volunteer Drives:

- Prepare volunteers to help local area drives. Whether it's giving food, cover, or basic reassurance, local area volunteers can have a massive effect.

8. Inclusivity:

- Guarantee inclusivity inside the local area. Backing and regard different voices and encounters to establish a climate where all individuals feel esteemed.

9. Observe Triumphs:

- Perceive and praise individual and local area triumphs. Uplifting feedback supports inspiration and builds up aggregate versatility.

10. Emotional Wellness Mindfulness Missions:

- Send off mindfulness crusades around emotional wellness. Lessening disgrace and advancing discourse can encourage psychological wellness versatility inside the local area.

11. Solid Administrations:

- Support people group pioneers who can direct and join the local area during testing times. Solid administration is significant for versatility.

12. Social Association Drives:

- Coordinate get-togethers and exercises that urge local area individuals to interface, offer, and back each other. Building a feeling of having a place is fundamental.

13. Social and Profound Help:

- Recognize the significance of social and otherworldly emotionally supportive networks inside the local area. Regard and celebrate social variety.

14. Standard Registrations:

- Execute standard registrations to screen the prosperity of local area individuals, especially during seasons of emergency or huge pressure.

15. resilience plans:

- Make resilience plans at the local area level, zeroing in on building an establishment for future difficulties.

Coping as a local area isn't just about turning around difficulty together but in addition about sustaining an aggregate soul of solidarity, solidarity, and backing. By meeting up and carrying out these procedures, networks can improve their versatility, guaranteeing that they are more ready to defeat difficulties and flourish even with difficulties.

CHAPTER 6
Techniques for Resilience.

Resilience is an expertise that can be developed and fortified. Here are procedures and systems to help you assemble and upgrade your strength:

1. Mindfulness:

- Begin by creating mindfulness. Figure out your assets, shortcomings, and how you commonly answer pressure and affliction. This mindfulness is the most vital phase in building flexibility.

2. Positive Self-Talk:

- Practice positive self-talk. Challenge negative or foolish considerations and supplant them with additional hopeful and valuable ones.

3. Critical thinking:

- Foster critical thinking abilities. Recognize the issues you face and work on tracking down functional arrangements. Break issues into reasonable moves to make them more receptive.

4. Versatility:

- Develop versatility. Perceive that change is a piece of life, and the capacity to adjust is a vital part of flexibility.

5. Adaptability:

- Be adaptable in your reasoning. Keep away from inflexible reasoning examples and be available to groundbreaking thoughts and ways to deal with critical thinking.

6. Solid Survival techniques:

- Take on solid survival techniques. Try not to depend on undesirable propensities like substance misuse and second thoughts go to better approaches to overseeing pressure, like activity or care.

7. Using time effectively:

- Further, develop time usage abilities. Focus on errands and put forth reasonable objectives to decrease the sensation of being overpowered.

8. Lay out Encouraging groups of people:

- Fabricate major areas of strength for an organization. Associate with companions friends and family who offer profound help and support.

9. Taking care of oneself:

- Focus on taking care of oneself. Take part in rehearses that advance your physical and mental prosperity, like standard activity, a reasonable eating regimen, and adequate rest.

10. Care and Reflection:

- Practice care and reflection. These procedures can assist you with remaining present, lessen pressure, and improve profound strength.

11. Look for Proficient Assistance:

- Feel free to proficient direction when required. Specialists, advisors, and mentors can offer master's help for building versatility.

12. Appreciation:

- Develop appreciation. Center around the positive parts of your life and express appreciation for individuals and encounters that enhance your life.

13. Gain from Affliction:

- Embrace misfortune as a chance for development. Consider what you can gain from testing encounters and how they can make you more grounded.

14. Put forth Reasonable Objectives:

- Put forth reasonable and attainable objectives. Achieving little objectives can support your certainty and add to your flexibility.

15. Keep a Feeling of Direction:

- Keep a feeling of direction. Take part in exercises that line up with your qualities and interests, as having a feeling of direction can improve versatility.

16. Keep Viewpoint:

- Keep up with a point of view. Recall that mishaps are much of the time brief, and a more extensive perspective on your life can assist you with exploring difficulties with no sweat.

17. Versatility Instruction:

- Think about searching out assets and training on building flexibility. Books, studios, and online courses can give important experiences and systems.

Building Resilience is a continuous excursion that includes creating mental and close-to-home strength. By ntegrating these methods into your life, you can fortify your capacity to
return from difficulty and flourish notwithstanding life's difficulties.

Problem-Solving Strategies for Building Resilience:

Powerful critical thinking is a vital part of versatility. Here are a few systems to assist you with handling difficulties and fabricating your critical thinking abilities:

1. Characterize the Issue:

- Characterize the issue you're confronting. Understanding the issue is the most vital phase in tracking down an answer.

2. Separate It:

- Partition the issue into more modest, more sensible parts. This makes it simpler to independently address every part.

3. Put forth Clear Objectives:

- Lay out clear and explicit objectives for tackling the issue. What is it that you need to accomplish? Characterize your targets.

4. Conceptualize Arrangements:

- Produce a rundown of likely arrangements. Try not to pass judgment or assess them at this stage; center around making a complete rundown.

5. Assess Choices:

- Assess every arrangement's advantages and disadvantages. Think about the possible results, dangers, and advantages of each methodology.

6. Pick the Best Arrangement:

- Select the arrangement that appears to be generally encouraging. Trust your judgment, however, be available to input from others.

7. Make an Arrangement:

- Foster a nitty gritty arrangement for executing the picked arrangement. Frame the means you want to take and set a course of events.

8. Make a move:

- Set your strategy in motion. Start dealing with the issue and venture out toward your answer.

9. Screen Progress:

- Consistently screen your advancement. Be adaptable and able to change your arrangement if fundamental.

10. Look for Help:

- Make sure to help or guidance from confided-in people or experts. Now and then, an external point of view can be important.

11. Self-Reflection:

- Consider your critical thinking process and the results. What functioned admirably? What could be improved for future difficulties?

12. Gain from Slip-ups:

- Embrace botches as learning amazing open doors. Cheer up by mishaps; all things being equal, use them to refine your critical thinking abilities.

13. Remain Positive:

- Keep a positive and hopeful mentality. An uplifting perspective can improve your resilience and imagination in critical thinking.

14. Endure:

- Be industrious and steady. Many difficulties demand investment and work to survive, so don't surrender without any problem.

15. Versatility:

- Be versatile in your critical thinking approach. If one arrangement doesn't work, attempt an alternate methodology.

16. Embrace Change:

- Be available to change and vulnerability. In some cases, issues can prompt positive changes in your day-to-day existence.

17. Fabricate Strength Assets:

- Fortify your general resilience through taking care of oneself, mindfulness, and encouraging groups of people. Strength is an establishment for viable critical thinking.

Powerful critical thinking is an expertise that can be created and refined over the long run. By applying these methodologies and persistently rehearsing your critical thinking skills, you can upgrade your versatility and explore life's difficulties with no sweat and certainty.

Coping with Stress and Anxiety: Strategies for Resilience.

Coping with pressure and tension is fundamental for building and keeping up with strength. Here are methodologies to assist you with dealing with these normal difficulties:

1. Care and Unwinding Strategies:

- Practice care contemplation and profound breathing activities. These strategies can assist you with remaining present at the time and lessen pressure and nervousness.

2. Active work:

- Participate in ordinary active work. Practice discharges endorphins, which are normal pressure relievers. It additionally advances better physical and psychological well-being.

3. Good dieting:

- Keep a fair eating regimen. Appropriate sustenance furnishes your body with the energy and supplements it requires to adapt to pressure and nervousness.

4. Rest:

- Focus on rest. Guarantee you get sufficient rest to assist your body with recuperating from everyday stressors.

5. Using time effectively:

- Further, develop time usage abilities. Focusing on undertakings and laying out reasonable objectives can decrease the sensation of being overpowered.

6. Social Help:
- Rest in your encouraging group of people. Talking about your thoughts with companions friends and family offers profound help and decreases nervousness.

7. Correspondence:
- Offer your viewpoints and feelings transparently. Suppressing sentiments can intensify pressure and nervousness.

8. Look for Proficient Assistance:
- Make it a point to proficient direction when required. Advisors, guides, or therapists can offer master support for overseeing pressure and tension.

9. Critical thinking:

- Foster critical thinking abilities to address the underlying drivers of stress and uneasiness.

10. Keep away from Compulsiveness:

- Discharge the requirement for flawlessness. Set sensible assumptions for you and acknowledge that nobody is awesome.

11. Put down Stopping points:

- Lay out sound limits to keep harmony between work, individual life, and taking care of oneself.

12. resilienceInstruction:

- Find out about resilience and stress the board through books, studios, and online courses.

13. Remain Positive:

- Develop an inspirational perspective on life. Center around arrangements as opposed to issues, and practice appreciation.

14. Mental Conduct Treatment (CBT):

- Consider CBT, a restorative methodology that helps people reevaluate pessimistic idea designs and oversee tension successfully.

15. Taking care of oneself:

- Focus on taking care of oneself practices, like getting some margin for side interests, unwinding, and exercises that give you pleasure.

16. Foster Survival techniques:

- Foster customized methods for dealing with stress that turn out best for you. This might incorporate innovative outlets, side interests, or unwinding methods.

17. Perceive Triggers:

- Recognize your pressure and uneasiness triggers. Understanding what causes these feelings is the most important phase in overseeing them.

18. Acknowledge Vulnerability:

- Embrace vulnerability as a piece of life. Not all things can be controlled or anticipated, and that is completely fine.

Coping with pressure and tension is a continuous interaction that requires mindfulness and practice. By applying these systems and looking for help when required, you can deal with these difficulties successfully, fabricate strength, and lead a more adjusted and satisfying life.

Finding Meaning in Adversity: A Resilience Booster.

Finding importance in misfortune is a strong method for upgrading your resilience and profound prosperity. This is the way you can find reason and importance in testing times:

1. Self-Reflection: Find an opportunity to think about your encounters and the difficulty you've confronted. What have you gained from these difficulties? What values have become more obvious to you?

2. Look for the Silver Linings: Search for the positive parts of tough spots. Difficulty can frequently prompt self-awareness, new open doors, and expanded mindfulness.

3. Embrace Development: Comprehend that self-improvement frequently emerges from affliction. Embrace the possibility that difficulties can be impetuses for personal growth.

4. Reconsider Needs: Difficulty can provoke you to rethink your needs and spotlight the main thing throughout everyday life. This can prompt a more significant and reason-driven presence.

5. Help other people: Finding importance can emerge out of helping other people who are going through comparative difficulties. Thoughtful gestures and support can give a feeling of direction.

6. Interface with Values: Reconnect with your guiding principles and convictions.

Adjusting your activities to your qualities can give a feeling of significance and satisfaction.

7. Put forth Objectives: Lay out significant objectives that line up with your qualities and yearnings. Pursuing these goals can provide you with a feeling of motivation.

8. Develop Strength Assets: Fortify your general versatility through taking care of oneself, mindfulness, and encouraging groups of people. resilience is an establishment for tracking down significance in difficulty.

9. Acknowledge Defect: Comprehend that life is defective, and difficulty is a piece of the human experience. Tolerating this blemish can prompt more noteworthy flexibility.

10. Self-Sympathy: Practice self-sympathy. Indulge yourself with a similar benevolence and understanding you would propose to a companion confronting difficulties.

11. Care: Embrace care and remain present at the time. Zeroing in on the present time and place can assist you with valuing life's little delights.

12. Gain from Difficulty: Consider what you can gain from troublesome encounters. How have they formed you, and how might you utilize this information to see it as significant?

13. Interface with Others: Look for help and association with other people who have confronted comparable difficulties. Shared encounters can give a feeling of local area and understanding.

14. Appreciation: Practice appreciation for the positive parts of your life. Perceiving the great can assist you with tracking down significance and reason in difficulty.

15. Embrace Change: Be available to change and vulnerability. Once in a while, moves lead to positive changes in your day-to-day existence.

Finding significance in difficulty is an individual and continuous excursion. It includes perceiving the examples, development, and open doors that emerge from difficulties. By applying these techniques and rehearsing self-reflection, you can uncover reason and importance in even the toughest spots, at last upgrading your versatility and prosperity.

CONCLUSIONS.

In the excursion of life, resilience is the key that opens our capacity to make due, yet to flourish despite misfortune. It's the ability to return, adjust, and develop further when going up against life's preliminaries. All through this investigation of versatility, we've revealed a heap of methodologies and procedures to assist you with building, sustaining, and fortifying your strength.

From understanding the foundations of difficulty to figuring out how to adapt to pressure and nervousness, every part of resilience has been tended to. We've dove into the significance of connections, self-sympathy, and the job of the local area in strength. We've additionally investigated the science behind resilience and how to track down the importance of misfortune.

resilience is an expertise that can be developed, and it flourishes in the prolific soil of mindfulness, idealism, and an encouraging group of people. It's sustained through care, appreciation, and the ability to adjust to change. Whether you're confronting individual difficulties or exploring the constantly changing scene of our reality, these devices and experiences can assist you with exploring with more noteworthy strength and self-restraint.

Recollecting that building strength isn't tied in with keeping away from troubles; it's tied in with embracing them as any open doors for development. As you push ahead throughout everyday life, realize that you can endure affliction as well as rise out of it smarter, more grounded, and stronger. The way may not generally be simple, yet it is without a doubt worth the excursion.

Eventually, versatility is a deep-rooted pursuit, and you can shape it. As you proceed to create and apply these techniques, may you track down the solidarity to confront life's difficulties with a feeling of versatility and a steady assurance to flourish.

ISBN 9798866666973
90000
9 798866 666973

PREVENTION IS BETTER. GET HELP!

Cerebrovascular chronicles

Causes

Brain disfunction

(stroke)

Cerebrum disorders

Effects of the diseases

DISEASE

ealing with stroke prevention ,causes and control

Raphel Bowston